Sponsored in honor of the great work of
Rabbi Yosef and Mrs. Rivka Shtrocks
of Chabad of Olympia WA.

Who Needs You

First Edition — 5780 / 2020
Copyright © 2020 by It's Good to Know Publishing
ALL RIGHTS RESERVED

Editor: Baily Friedman
Managing Editor: Rabbi Zalman Friedman
Design/Layout: Moshe Cohen

ISBN: 978-0-9862770-4-7
Paperback Edition: 5780 / 2020

ISBN: 978-0-922613-66-3
(Original Hardcover Edition)

It's Good to Know Publishing
860 Eastern Parkway #2, Brooklyn NY 11213
800-656-5669
For bulk orders and dedication opportunities
please contact zalman@itsgoodtoknow.org

www.itsgoodtoknow.org

The Rabbi Manis Friedman Children's Book Series

WHO NEEDS YOU

by Sara Blau

illustrated by
Aliza Boroda

IT'S GOOD TO
KNOW

The books are closed – we're finished writing,
School is done! It's so exciting!
We learned so much in class today,
But now we're heading home to play.

CLUB HOUSE

We reach my yard in
record timing,
I'm the first one,
climbing, climbing.

Up to the clubhouse
in the tree,
My friends come
zooming after me!

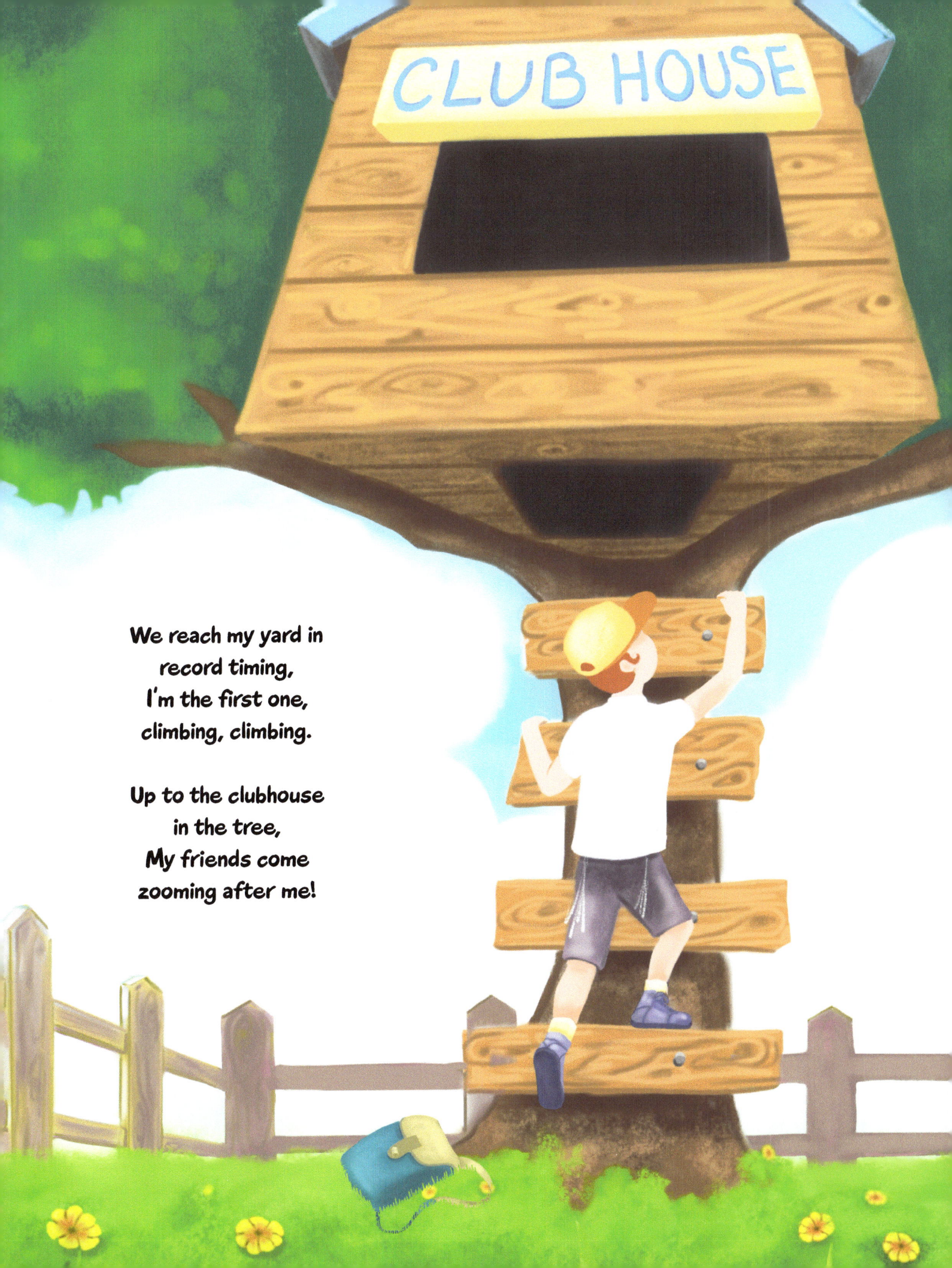

On the shelves are trains and tracks,
Cars and books and blocks in stacks,
Walkie-talkies, locks and keys,
And lights to shine on other trees.

We settle in,
and then I say,
"What do you think
we should do today?

"We can do what we want
and feel so free,
I'm glad to have you in my tree!"

CLUB HOUSE

So as I'm sitting
with the boys,
We hear my Zaidy's
booming voice.

"Chaim, Chaim,
excuse me please.
But after all,
whose trees are these?

"I'm sure you know what the answer is,
Hashem is the One; these trees are HIS!"

"Dear children,"
said my **Zaidy**, grinning,
"What was here
way in the beginning?

"Nothing at all,
no land or air,
Nothing until Hashem
put it there."

"You all knew that,
but did you know why?
Why did Hashem make
the earth and the sky?

"It's because He needs me,
and because He needs you,
And He needs all the mitzvos
that you and I do!

"And Hashem keeps creating,
He creates and creates.

"He watches us closely
and waits and waits,
For us to fulfill
His deepest needs
By keeping His mitzvos and
doing good deeds."

I turned to my Zaidy with a happy cry,
"Can my mitzvos bring joy to Hashem up so high?
Is that really true? Can that really be?
Does Hashem care that much about a kid like me?"

"That's right!" says Zaidy, "It's truer than true,
Hashem is depending on the mitzvos you do!
He made this world, and the heavens, too
Just so His mitzvos could be done by YOU."

At home and at school, all the Torah I'm learning,
Is never about what reward I'm earning.

"Hashem, all these mitzvos that I do –
Are really and truly, just for YOU!"

Then once again,
we're climbing, climbing,
But our goal has changed
with record timing.

Hashem is the most
important One,
We've got to get
His mitzvos done!

Giving people
a friendly greeting,
Brachos on the food
we're eating,

Letting others
choose the game,
Help them practice
flawless aim.

In my pushka
coins are clanging,
Mezuzos on my
doors are hanging.

Every mitzvah
is a precious gem
That is so important
to Hashem!

CLUB HOUSE

We take turns
to show we're caring,
Speak with kindness,
spend time sharing.

Feel the thrill
of being free
To do His mitzvos,
you and me!

My friends and I are playing, when,
We hear my Zaidy's voice again,
"I have a nice surprise for you,
It's for your whole clubhouse crew!"

Here comes Zaidy, up the ladder,
He made us a sign – we're so flattered!
"Let's hang this up right away,
Words to remember every day."

Glossary

Hashem .... God, Creator

Mezuzos .... Small scroll put onto the door post

Mitzvos .... G-d's Needs

Pushka .... Charity Box

Torah .... Bible

Zaidy .... Grandfather